The Inevitable Zero

The Inevitable Zero

Kaushik Acharya

HAWAKAL PUBLISHERS

Published by Subhra Chakraborty on behalf of
Hawakal Publishers, 185, Kali Temple Road,
Nimta, Calcutta 700049

Cover texture source: Dreamstime dot com

Cover concept and design: Chitrangi

Copyright 2017 © Kaushik Acharya

First edition [Paperback]: August 2017

ISBN-13: 978-81-934230-9-7

Price: INR 225 | US Dollar 8.00

Dedicated to my mentor,
Professor Debarchana Sarkar

Department of Sanskrit
Jadavpur University
Calcutta

Contents

Introduction

I had a quiet and rush-free childhood. I can remember the day Baba bought me a slate-board and chalk-pencil. He also bought a copy of *Barnoparichoy*, which is considered the first book to a Bengali child. I wondered how effortlessly Baba taught me the lessons from the book. I had to learn the Bengali letters ক, খ, গ, ঘ (*Ka, Kha, Ga, Gha*) and the Bengali numbers ১, ২, ৩, ৪ (1,2,3,4) first. Baba advised me to use my fingers as I learned the numbers. Baba told me that 2 was larger than 1, 3 was larger than 2, and so on. As a curious child I asked him, "Is the zero the largest number?" I don't remember his answer now. However, after a few months I got to understand the meaning of the zero (0) as it was situated after the nine (9). It was not the zero but the 10 (ten). In those days the zero was just a number. In my high-school days I found the zero scary. There was always a chance to get zero if had failed to solve a sum in Mathematics. Our teacher once told us that the zero could eat the rest of the numbers from being immensely powerful.

Being a student of Sanskrit language and literature I have been taught ancient Indian philosophy; we came to know of nothingness or emptiness that made up the core concept of the zero. I tried to grasp the internal meaning as laid in the philosophies of ancient Indian scriptures.

"The Hiranyagarbha Suktam," and "The Nassadiya Suktam," in *The Veda*s claim that nothingness or the zero exists everywhere—from the beginning of the universe until its end. According to the modern science it has been proved that there was nothing present during the initiation of the universe. I think the zero is the state of ultimate nothingness as all wisdoms lead to experiencing the nothingness — a feeling that makes you think that you are *shunya* — the zero.

The zero brings peace; it also brings a feeling of calmness and control over the 'self' and situations. This zero is the final understanding of the supreme wisdom. A zero-mind receives and accepts, hears and registers, and notes the critical points of life. It is the abode of peace and quietude. When we meditate we are advised to look into the zero and become free of all thoughts. It is that space where the enlightenment arrives.

The Bhagvad Gita and *The Vedas* talk about the universe being created from nothingness, *shunya* or the zero. God in His ambiguous form is also said to be *shunya*; and in His definite form He is called *ananta* or the infinite. Thus, from the zero comes infinity. It is considered a symbol of unity and also eternity. The zero is related to the ideas of *samadhi*, *amaratva*, *Brahma*, among others. The objective of yogic practices is to unite the individual self with *Brahma*, which is the Absolute Reality. According to the Hindu scriptures *Brahma* is devoid of any attributes; since the zero or *shunya* has no attributes *Brahma* is also referred to as *shunya*. Oneness of the 'self' with the cosmic self is called *samadhi*, which in itself is *shunya*. Practicing yoga leads the mind to *shunya* by releasing ego, desires and attachments.

Understanding *shunya* leads to spiritual liberation. While writing a paper on "Science and Technology in Ancient India" the idea of theorizing the zero appeared in my mind. In Mathematics the zero is used in several ways. As I began to write I found some misconceptions on the internet; even a few books on Mathematics did not describe the zero in a proper way. I'm sure there are several studies that have dealt with the very notion; however, I have tried to explain and interpret the sources that revolve around the zero and its implications. Whether my take is unique can only be assessed by readers and scholars.

Kaushik Acharya
August 15, 2017
Coochbehar, West Bengal

Existential Invention

Was the zero invented or discovered? Before answering the question we must understand the difference between 'invention' and 'discovery.' Creating something new through the process of a new method, theory, formula, etc. is called 'invention,' whereas 'discovery' is a search or re-search of a thing which already exists, or it is inventing something that is present among us, but the society is not aware of the thing. For example, Newton discovered the theory of gravitation but the gravitational science continues to exist since the birth of the universe. The theory of gravitation is called Newton's discovery; not invention. Again, if I may ask, did men invent the fire? Or did they discover it?

Most of the people would say the fire was discovered; probably because of the fact that the fire existed before we used it. The forest-fire can be cited as an example here. Similarly, people may urge that the numbers existed much before we learned to use them. But, what about a non-integer number like *pi*? It would seem unreasonable if I say *pi* was invented, as *pi* had a certain value even before we drew a circle for the first time. The diameter of a circle has always been *pi*. Inventions may have flaws, and we can work on them further to make things look better. In Nature the mathematical formulae work even before we realize how and when they work. According to many scholars the zero has been discovered. In fact, the entire numerical system and the concept of Mathematics have been discovered, not invented. But, the forms, especially the way we talk about Mathematics today, was invented. The formulae, as used in Mathematics, existed before, but in a different form altogether. We discovered them, gave them a definite form and standardized the formulae. Everything we learn in Mathematics has been inspired by the Nature, and our day-to-day activities. Like we have ten fingers, and thus, we invented the decimal notation.

There are more than one thought on who invented the zero, but before we get into the argument we must address the question: Was the zero invented or discovered? There are several views in this regard: Let me put it this way: If you have one apple in each hand, you got two apples in total. Whether you are aware of Mathematics or not, you won't possibly go wrong in determining the total number of apples you got. However, with the application of mathematical rule you later discover that the one (1) adds to the other one (1) to yield two (2).

Mathematics, the subject, dwells in a conceptual world; the numbers are attributes expressed in their physical manifestations. According to other scholars the concept of zero was invented as it did not exist before. In a way this is true, as the Nature never allows a "zero" in it. The notion of the zero has been created by human minds. We could have used any other symbol to represent nothingness. However, I can guess, ages ago someone chose to draw a figure that resembled an egg and named it "zero." We might have named it differently, and hence, we invented the zero. The scholars consider

Mathematics an invention, and the same holds true for the zero. Mathematics, as some teachers say, is not "science," but a language used to explore the mysteries of science and Nature.

But, why are we emphasizing on invention? If we had only a thumb in each hand, we would have required a binary notation of representing the numbers, and thus, we would have invented it. The humans invented the concept of the zero in order to understand Mathematics and the principles of the Universe better. Again, we needed the zero; we needed to count on the emptiness, and thus, we invented the zero. Moreover, we created the zero to keep an account of the numbers or their absence!

Necessity is the mother of invention, they say. "Invention" and "Discovery" bear the same meaning, but they do not necessarily carry the same relevance. One invents something that did not previously exist. On the other hand, we discover a thing that already existed. We can say, the zero was invented, but I will prefer to put it this way: The zero holds fair similarity with "virtual reality," which means "not physically existing as such, but made by a software to appear to do so." I'll name the phenomena (invention of the zero) "existential invention."

The Inventor(s)

The main objective of Vedic literature is to describe the glory of the Creator and his immense prowess. The visions of the Vedic sages, as discussed in Vedic literature, have been meticulous, vast and related to the Nature and material world. *The Veda*s are the first texts in the literature of the human race. They deal with knowledge, both physical and spiritual. The Vedic views revolve around the concept of Nature and life. We can easily figure out how the Nature was related to the life and livelihood of the Vedic people through their literature that is referred to as *The Veda*. *The Veda*s are the compilation of *Mantra*s. The sciences, which are connected to the human civilizations, have germinated from the same *Mantra*s. Thus, the source and history of the natural sciences (like medicinal science, mathematics, geometry, etc.) are believed to have originated from *The Veda*s. If ancient wisdom is considered, we would find that sage *Atharban* first discovered the fire, while *Dirghatama* invented the longest method of measuring the time. *Garg* introduced astronomy, *Lagadh* astrology, and the great sage, *Kanad*, introduced the atomic science. *Bhardvaj* was the one who introduced the herbal sciences; *Atreya* is considered the father of pharmacology, and *Sushruta* the father of the surgical sciences. *Medhatithi* introduced *arithmetic*, *Boudhayana* geometry, and *Aryabhatta* was the first to invent algebra, and later he used the zero (0) for the first time, but the concept of nothingness existed before, especially in the Vedic literature.

The zero is considered the symbol of the amorphous *Brahma* or infinite. It is said that the universe has been derived from the zero, and finally, everything dissolves into it. The globe is almost round in shape. The sky, horizon, and the earth appear roundish. The sensory gateways of the human body are round as well. The Vedic literature says the zero is smaller than micro-subtle and bigger than the magnificent. When placed before the one (1), the zero makes no difference; however, when placed after the one, the value of the constant number, one, becomes tenfold. The concept of the zero, as introduced by the Vedic sages, is worthy enough, but unfortunately, some scholars fail to acknowledge the wisdom nurtured in ancient India, for they are either unaware of or show ignorance to the philosophies as laid down in *The Veda*s and *The Upanishad*s. They tend to refer *Aryabhatta* (Fifth-century AD), the famous Indian mathematician, to as the inventor of the zero and the decimal method. The authenticity of the several internet sources (like Wikipedia, etc.) is debatable in this context.

According to *Wikipedia* we are yet to confirm the name of the inventor, the one who invented the zero, but it has been established globally that the invention took place in India. However, there are other stories that claim that the invention occurred first in the Babylonian period. The *Wikipedia* also says about the people of *Maya* civilization who supposedly invented the zero. But, these stories have failed to influence the scholars as the Vedic Aryans (the Hindus) have been given the due credit to have invented the zero in India. As a matter of fact, the *Wikipedia* fails to address the question: How did the Vedic Aryans come to know about the zero?

Although the *Wikipedia* has admitted that the zero was invented in India "for the third time," but they did not acknowledge the Vedic sages, they have rather bestowed the credit to *Aryabhatta* (Fifth-century AD) later in their discussions. The *Wikipedia* emphasized on the Babylon and *Maya* civilizations probably from being a Western-world organization! What depresses me most is even a few Indian organizations blindly follow the Western school of thought and mimic the *Wikipedia*. They don't want to explore the truth as laid down in our ancient scriptures.

The *Paravigyan* goes ahead of the *Wikipedia* and they think it is wrong to say that the Indians discovered the zero. According to them it will be proper to claim that the Indians have discovered the modern numbering system. Prior to the discovery of this system in India, there were different systems of calculation in every civilization and country, and all of them had their own method of marking the ten (10), the base number. However, in the *Maya* civilization the base number was said to be the twenty (20).

The *Paravigyan* denies the evidences, which have been present in *The Vedas*, they admitted. They sound contradictory as they say some people also have the illusion that this method of zero was discovered in the Vedic period and that there is evidence of this in *The Vedas* itself. This is absolutely wrong.

The *Paravigyan* continues to disseminate ambiguous information:

> *Aryabhatta* (476 AD) did not discover this new system. This search had already happened before him. From his book it is known that *Aryabhatta* was well-versed with this method. *Aryabhatta* gave birth to a new alphabetic method. He has also

worked in his book, *Aryabhatiya*, in the same method, not in the new system.

Yes, why the scholars do consider *Aryabhatta* as the discoverer of the zero lies in the fact that in his book, *Aryabhatiya* (498 AD), *Aryabhatta* noted the numbers from one to the billion. While presenting the series of the ten (like 10, 100, 1000, 10,000, among other numbers in the series) he opined: "स्थानात् स्थानं दशगुणं स्यात" (Each number is ten-time bigger than the previous number). The scholars of Indian Mathematics, due to their lack of interest in ancient Indian literature, remain confused, and hardly re-search the data as available on the Internet.

The worshipers of the Nature used to watch the spherical sun in the sky, and the secrets of the universe unveiled before them one after another. *The Chhandogyopanishad* expresses this mystery and says the sun is *Brahma*. Firstly he was *asat* (incomprehensible) and then he turned *sat* (comprehensible). The sun first became an egg and got split into two parts. The silver part became *pritviloka* (the earth), and the gold part became the *dyuloka* (the zone that exists beyond the sky).

आदित्यो ब्रह्मेत्यादेशस्तस्योपव्याख्यानम् असदेवेद
मग्र आसीत्
तत्सदासीत्तत्सदासीत् तत्समभवत्तदाण्डं निरवर्तत त
त्संवत्सरस्य मात्रामशयत तन्निरभिद्यत ते आण्ड
कपाले रजतं च सुवर्णं चाभवताम्
—छान्दोग्योपनिषद् (3.19.1)

[Translation: The sun is *Brahma*: this is the teaching. An explanation thereof follows: In the beginning this universe was non-existent. It became existent. It grew. It turned into an egg. The egg lay for the period of a year. Then it broke open. Of the two halves of the egg-shell, one half was of silver, the other of gold.]

The zero has its resemblance with the shape of an egg. The story, as depicted in the verses above, on the origin of the universe later became popular in Babylon, Egypt, Iran, Greece, among other countries. In Greek mythology *Khannaas* and *Adrasteia* produced a huge egg that split to become the sky (from the upper part of the egg) and the earth (from the lower part of the egg).

On the other hand, in Milton's *Paradise Lost* it is imagined that God's bird, "Spirit," spreading its large feathers while sitting on the huge zero, which was perhaps inspired by *Suparna* (the sun-bird) of *The Rigveda*[1,2] (5.47.3, 10.177.1), and these metaphors (Spirit and *Suparna*) were used in the context of the sun.

The Bible says: In the beginning of creation there was darkness above the deep and the *Spirit of God* moved upon the waters in the void earth (Genesis 1.2). Thus, the emergence of the sun, eliminating the darkness, is very similar as in *The Rigveda*.

The creation of the universe from the spherical sun has been a scientific fact, which went to other civilizations from the Vedic Aryans. One should remember that the philosophical interpretations of the ancient scriptures have lead to the invention of the zero first, which in turn lead to the formation of Indian Mathematical Sciences.

Notes:

The Rigveda[1, 2]

उक्षा समुद्रो अरुषः सुपर्णः पूर्वस्य योनिं पितुरा
विवेश।
मध्ये दिवो निहितः पृश्निरश्मा वि चक्रमे
रजसस्पात्यन्तौ॥

—ऋग्वेद (5.47.3)

[Translation: The *mantra* says about the sun-bird. It flies extremely fast and always shines bright in resplendent light. The bird has strong wings … helps in rain … pleases the gods. Like the father it went to the east and the rest followed which was comprised of several colors as contained in the heaven. The sun followed the colors and emerged to protect the world.]

पतंगमक्तमसुरस्य मायया हृदा पश्यन्ति मनसा
विपश्चितः।
समुद्रे अन्तः कवयो वि चक्षते मरीचीनां
पदमिच्छन्ति वेधसः॥

—ऋग्वेद (10.177.1)

[Translation: After much discussion, mentally, the wise men visualized a flyer! The flyers, as they saw, were infiltrated by the demonic *maya*. The sages found the incident occurring in the ocean and the flyers got the desire to reach out to the abode of divine light.]

The Formation

The *Brihadaranyakopanishad* has expressed the zero as पूर्ण (complete), which proves the mutual relation of *Brahma* and the material world. The argumentative linguistics employed by the *Upanishadic* sages was later translated into the scientific terminology the Mathematicians have used to determine the numerical value of the zero.

ॐ पूर्णमदः पूर्णमिदं पूर्णात्पूर्णमुदच्यते।
पूर्णस्य पूर्णमादाय पूर्णमेवावशिष्यते॥
—बृहदारण्यकोपनिषद् (5.1.1)

[Translation: That *Brahma* is complete; this world is also complete. This complete world was created by the absolute *Brahma*. The absolute *Brahma* remains the only being if the world, which is also complete, is separated from that absolute being.]

In the Vedic period the word ख (*kha*) symbolized the zero:

ॐ खं ब्रह्म खं पुराणं वायुरं खमिति ह स्माह
कौरव्याणीपुत्रो वेदो यं ब्राह्मणा विदुर्वेदैनेन
यद्वेदितव्यम्।

—बृहदारण्यकोपनिषद् (5.1.1)

[Translation: *Om* is the *Brahma*, the eternal
ether (*kha*). 'The ether containing air,' says the
son of *Kauravyayani*. *The Veda* is meant for the
*Brahmana*s (knowers of *Brahma*), who
understand that by studying *The Veda* the
learner comes to know of what is to be
learned.]

This is to be noted that the
mantra, as mentioned above, bears the
word *kha* that symbolized the zero, which
also depicted fullness. According to this
mantra, *Brahma* is ख (*kha*) and according to
the scripture, *The Brihadaranyakkopanishad*,
the son of the sage *Kaurabyani* is considered
the pioneer of *kha*-tenet.

This *mantra* is considered to be
the first mathematical formula that defined
the principle of the Vedic zero; later the
Indian mathematicians adopted the word
kha as the definition of the same.

ख शब्देन शून्यमुच्यते।
—लीलावती, शून्यपरिकर्म

[Translation: The zero is called by the word *kha*.]

*The Veda*s or *The Upanishad*s have described the emergence of *sat* objects from the *asat* objects, and in due course the concept of the zero has merged with the discussions on the sky, *Brahma*, *Vyom* and water. *Bhaskaracharya* presented a strong definition of the zero in his book, *Leelavati*, which is said to be the demotic mathematical version of the *mantra* पूर्णमदः पूर्णमिदम्...

योगे खं क्षेपसमं, वर्गादौ
खं खभाजितो राशिः।
खहरः स्यात् खगुणः खं
खगुणश्चिन्त्यश्चशेषविधौ॥
शून्ये गुणके जाते खं
हारश्चेत पुनस्तदा राशिः।
विकृत एव ज्ञेयस्तथैव
खेनोनितश्च युतः॥

—लीलावती, शून्यपरिकर्म (45.46)

The *shloka* means the sum is equal to the number upon adding a number to the zero. The root of the zero is also zero. Dividing a number by the zero results in the same numerical figure, and such a number, as no (zero) change occurs, is referred to as *khahara* (खहर). When someone multiplies a number with zero it yields zero. Similarly, no (zero) change happens when the zero is added to a number, or if zero is subtracted from a number.

kham, khe and *khaani* (खम्, खे, खानि): the singular, dual and plural forms respectively of the word, *kha* (ख), have been used many a time in *The Rigveda*. Any object which is spherical or porous was called *kha* (ख) by the Vedic sages. The outlets that helped in the passage of water from the clouds and glaciers were considered spherical, and thus, they were called *kha*. The Space is also said to be round-shaped, and hence, it is called *kha*. Similarly, the circular wheels of a chariot and their central points were also called

kha. The following *mantra*s of *The Rigveda*[1]
are relevant in this context:

खं वेपसा तुविजात स्तवानः —ऋग्वेद (4.11.2)

अङ्घि खं वर्तया —ऋग्वेद (10.156.3)

वृत्रहाखिदत्खे अरां इव खेदया —ऋग्वेद (8.77.3)

खे रथस्य खे अनसः खे युगस्य शतक्रतो

—ऋग्वेद (8.91.7)

वज्रेण खान्यतृणन्नदीनाम् —ऋग्वेद (2.15.3)

सिन्धूनपावृणोदपिहितेव खानि —ऋग्वेद (4.28.1)

अदर्दरुत्समसृजो वि खानि —ऋग्वेद (5.32.1)

अन्वपां खान्यतन्तमोजसा —ऋग्वेद (7.82.3)

The Vedic implication of the
word, *kha*, as found in *The Samaveda*, *The
Yajurveda* and *The Atharvaveda*, bears the
same relevance as that in *The Rigveda*.

In *The Atharvaveda* (10.2.1) the
sense organs having oval holes have been
called *khaani* (खानि), which is the plural
form of *kha* (ख), and the seven (सप्त)
organs have been stated as
Saptakhaani (सप्तखानि) in *The Atharvaveda*

(10.2.6). The fortieth chapter of *The Yajurveda* that is called *Isoponisad* or *Ishavasayopanishad* is important in this context, as *kha* has been used to denote *Brahma* for the first time:

ॐ खं ब्रह्म [यजुर्वेद (40.7)]

The universe would not have existed had there been no zero (nothingness). According to "The Hiranyagarbha Suktam" in *The Rigveda* (10.121) *Hiranyagarbha* is considered the first-ever creation. It was zero-shaped. The same zero got bigger, and finally formed *maha-shunya* (the space). The entire universe is situated in this *maha-shunya*. The *Hiranyagarbha* has been considered as the oval-shaped uterus of both the living creatures and the world. It was worshiped by the names of *Brahmaa*, *Vishnu*, *Shiva* and among others.

The origin of Indian cosmology emerged from the philosophical sources of *The Rigveda* and from them the philosophical features of the concept of the zero began to evolve. One of the objectives of the philosophical hymns in *The Rigveda* is to unveil the mystery of the transformation from *asat* (non-existent) object to *sat* (existent) object with the help of algebra. According to *The Rigveda* the Almighty arrived first as *Hiranyagarbha,* the golden egg, and then, God upheld the earth and *dyuloka. Hiranyagarbha,* otherwise called *Prajapati,* has been addressed by the letter, *ka* (क), as follows:

हिरण्यगर्भः समवर्तताग्रे भूतस्य जातः पतिरेक आसीत्।

स दाधार पृथिवीं द्यामुतेमां कस्मै देवाय हविषा विधेम॥

—ऋग्वेद (10.121.1)

[Translation: In the beginning of creation, *Hiranyagarbha* was born; when born, he was the only Lord (sustainer and nourisher) of all created beings. He held together this earth and the heaven. We propitiate That Lord *ka,* with oblations. (Or, What other God than *Prajapati* shall we adore with our oblations?)]

The *Vedic* Aryans treated *ka* as the creator of the entire universe. *Sayanacharya,* among other commentators, has described *Hiranyagarbha* in the light of *ka.*

कस्मै। अत्र किंशब्दोऽनिर्ज्ञातस्वरूपत्वात् प्रजापतौ
वर्तते। यद्वा सृष्टयर्थं कामयत इति कः।

—सायणभाष्यम् (10.121.1)

The tradition to accept the sun
or the other stars as *kha* was very old to
the Aryans. In order to unite the two
concepts, *ka* and *kha*, some mathematical
equations of algebra were used in the
Upanishadic times. But, the philosophers
were puzzled as to how *kha*, which was
derived from *ka*, could become *ka* again?

Advaita Vedanti (*The Vedanta* is the
concluding text of *The Veda*. *The Vedanta*
endorses monism, which means a state
where duality does not exist anymore.
Philosophers and sages who followed the
tenets of *The Vedanta* are known as *Advaita
Vedanti*) *Shankaracharya*, among others had
written several commentaries on the
mystery; however, *The Chhandogyopanishad*
solved the puzzle logically with its
mathematical approach.

कं ब्रह्म खं ब्रह्म...कं तदेव खं यदेव

—छान्दोग्योपनिषद् (4.10.5)

The *shloka* means both *ka* and *kha* are the two forms of *Brahma*. They mean the same. In Vedic philosophy all contradictions have thus been resolved.

The Rigveda was the most ancient scripture to the Aryans. If we study the *mantra*s of *The Rigveda* we can see there are praises for many gods and goddesses. *The Rigveda* is based on polytheism, but the tenth *mandala* (chapter), which is the final chapter of *The Rigveda,* surprisingly turns towards monotheism. Later in the *Upanishadic* period the philosophers had turned monotheism into nihilism or absolutism through mathematical equations. Nihilism or absolutism of the *Upanishad*s is closely linked to monotheistic *Brahma* by its *maya*-power. Thus, it is more appropriate to refer nihilism to as theism or dualistic nihilism. However, it can be differentiated from the Buddhist nihilism. The great ancient Indian poet in Sanskrit language and literature, *Kalidasa*, had linked the concept of this cosmology to the *shabda* (word) and *artha* (meaning) with his belief on *Parvati-Parameshswarou* (lord *Shiva* and his wife, goddess *Parvati).*

वागर्थाविव संपृक्तौ वागर्थप्रतिपत्तये।
जगतः पितरौ वन्दे पार्वतीपरमेश्वरौ॥

—रघुवंशम् (1.1)

[Translation: The parents of the universe, *Shiva* and *Parvati*, are attached to each other as the word is attached to its meaning. To get the word and the meaning, I (*Kalidasa*) am worshipping you both.]

In mathematical terms, it is the union of *ka* and *kha* that leads to the creation of the universe. Indian mythology suggests that *Shiva* is the destroyer; hence, he is represented by the word *kha,* as destruction leads to zero-existence of the creation. On the other hand, *Parvati* nurtures the creation and she is represented by the word *ka.* Both *Shiva* and *Parvati* merge to become one and thus, the creation (the world) emerges from the one (1) that has its roots in the zero (0). Therefore, the above-mentioned *sholka* happens to be an advance indication of the numbers zero and one.

In order to understand the above-mentioned mathematics on the mysteries of the creation, we need to grasp the *Upanishadic* cosmology and investigate it thoroughly. On the surface of the cosmology, until the monotheistic *Brahma* unites with *maya* and exhibits duality, the emergence of the mathematical process of becoming the *kha* (which is *Brahma* along with *maya*, otherwise called *Saguna Brahma*) from the *ka* (which also is *Brahma* but devoid of *maya* and thus, it is called *Nirguna Brahma*) does not take place.

Notes: *The Rigveda*[1]

Only the complete *mantra*s have been cited here. The use of *kham*, *khe*, *khani* need to be understood in the mantras and hence, their translations have been avoided.

वि षाह्यग्ने गृणते मनीषां खं वेपसा तुविजात स्तवानः।
विश्वेभिर्यद्वावनः शुक्र देवैस्तन्नो रास्व सुमहो भूरि मन्म॥
—ऋग्वेद (4.11.2)

आग्ने स्थूरं रयिं भर पृथुं गोमन्तमश्विनम्।
अङ्धि खं वर्तया पणिम्॥

—ऋग्वेद (10.156.3)

समितान्वृत्रहाखिदत्खे अराँ इव खेदया।
प्रवृद्धो दस्युहाभवत्॥

—ऋग्वेद (8.77.3)

खे रथस्य खेऽनसः खे युगस्य शतक्रतो।
अपालामिन्द्र त्रिष्पूत्व्यकृणोः सूर्यत्वचम्॥

—ऋग्वेद (8.91.7)

सद्मेव प्राचो वि मिमाय मानैर्वज्रेण
खान्यतृणन्नदीनाम्।
वृथासृजत्पथिभिर्दीर्घयाथैः सोमस्य ता मद
इन्द्रश्चकार॥

—ऋग्वेद (2.15.3)

त्वा युजा तव तत्सोम सख्य इन्द्रो अपो मनवे
ससुतस्कः।
अहन्नहिमरिणात्सप्त सिन्धूनपावृणोदपिहितेव
खानि॥

—ऋग्वेद (4.28.1)

अदर्दरुत्समसृजो वि खानि त्वमर्णवान्बद्बधानाँ
अरम्णाः।
महान्तमिन्द्र पर्वतं वि यद्वः सृजो वि धारा अव
दानवं हन्॥
—ऋग्वेद (5.32.1)

अन्वपां खान्यतृन्तमोजसा सूर्यमैरयतं दिवि प्रभुम्।
इन्द्रावरुणा मदे अस्य मायिनोऽपिन्वतमपितः
पिन्वतं धियः॥
—ऋग्वेद (7.82.3)

The *Ka* and the *Kha*

Creation is a dynamic process. For any kind of creation it is needed to keep changing from one form to another. The *Kutastha Brahma* is changeless and impartial, and thus, for researchers of cosmology it can't be a reason toward the creation of the universe. But, when it intends to create, it (commonly referred to as "he") has to take refuge in *maya*. In such a state of communion, *Kutastha Brahma* is known by several names: God, *Saguna Brahma, Shiva, Maheshwara,* among others. A *sadhak* (one who does religious practices and follows rituals) who worships *maya* as the goddess of the divine light, practically worships goddess *Durga* or *Mahakali,* among other deities.

According to the *Shaktatantra,* a banyan seed holds the future banyan tree in a subtle way. Similarly, the primordial energy (represented as a dot) of the inner world (soul) forms a divine triangle (*yoni*).

यथा न्यग्रोधबीजस्थः शक्तिरूपो महाद्रुमः।
तथा हृदयबीजस्थं जगदेतच्चराचरम्॥
—पराप्रावेशिका, क्षेमराज

कालेन भिद्यमानस्तु स बिन्दुर्भवति त्रिधा॥

—प्रपञ्चसार तन्त्र (1.42)

The *Shvetashvataropanishad* says this dual presence of *Prakriti* (Nature) and *Purusha* (Human) is the combination of *maya* and *Maheshwara*, or *Parvati* and *Parameswara*. As they are inter-connected, they cannot be separated from each other. *The Upanishad* denotes *maya* as the supreme Nature and its deity as *Maheswara* or *Brahma*. The entire universe is in sync with the duality, under the shadow of *Purusha* and *Prakriti*—

मायां तु प्रकृतिं विद्यान्मायिनं तु महेश्वरम्।

तस्यावयवभूतैस्तु व्याप्तं सर्वमिदं जगत्॥

—श्वेताश्वतरोपनिषद् (4. 10)

As stated in the previous chapter, *Kalidasa* has also reflected on the cosmology in the form of *Parvati-Parameshwarau*, who was considered the parent of the world. In the *Upanishadic* era the cosmologists realized that the genesis of the world was made possible by the merger of both *Brahma* (*Shiva*) and *Shakti*, the *Prana*-energy.

We must note that *Shiva* and *Shakti* are the synonyms of the *kha* and *ka* respectively. Indian cosmology believes that the chaos (*Saguna Brahma*) remains unchanged until they unite. But, after their union they create the universe. The word 'chaos' is an English word derived from the Greek word, *Khaios*. Interestingly, on the surface of Indo-European linguistics, the *Vedic* cosmology accepts the similarity of the *ka* and *kha*.

The Chhandogyopanishad claims that the *ka* and the *kha* are similar, and the teachings reached Greece. In *The Bible* "chaos" was used to denote ancient water of the creation. In *Paradise Lost* Milton wrote that the heaven and the earth were born from "chaos."

The Decimal System

We see a similarity in Indian cosmology and Vedic calculation system. The value (number) of *ka* is one (1) and *kha* is zero (0). Although in terms of mathematical values both are different, however, they are interdependent and integral too. Without the zero the one (1) cannot form further numbers (like 10, 100, 1000, and so on), and without the zero the one becomes insignificant. As soon as they get a chance to adapt to the strength of the decimal numbers, the ability to create and calculate begins to grow further.

The invention of the decimal number system is related to the invention of the zero, as found in the philosophical hymns of *The Rigveda*. Hence, it becomes evident that with the emergence of the zero in the "Nasadiya Suktam," "Hiranyagarbha Suktam," "Purusha Suktam, "among others, the one (1) gets the chance to become ten (10), one-hundred (100), one-thousand (1000), and so on; the reason being the decimal method. In "Hiranyagarbha Suktam"

Prajapati has been praised by the letter, *ka*, which points to the one (1) in terms of mathematics as discussed before.

हिरण्यगर्भः समवर्तताग्रे

भूतस्य जातः पतिरेक आसीत्।

स दाधार पृथिवीं द्यामुतेमां

कस्मै देवाय हविषा विधेम॥

—ऋग्वेद (10.121.1)

According to "The Nasadiya Suktam" in *The Rigveda* there was no *sat*, nor was there *asat* prior to the creation of the universe.

नासदासीन्नो सदासीत्तदानीं

नासीद्रजो नो व्योमा परो यत्।

—ऋग्वेद (10.129.1)

Even the sun, and other planets and the stars were non-existent during the inception of the greater universe. There was no air as well. This absence has been described by the word *kha* or the zero previously in this study. Surprisingly, the one and only *Brahma-tatva* (concept) was existent even without the air.

आनीदवातं स्वधया तदेकम्। —ऋग्वेद (10.129.2)

The sequence of cosmology-principle runs as follows: We get the number, one-thousand (1000), in the first *mantra*, "सहस्रशीर्षा पुरुषः..." in "The Purusha Suktam," another philosophical hymn of *The Rigveda*. An interesting example of the strength and scientific viability of the decimal method (about the one with the zero), is found in the following *mantra* in "The Purusha Suktam." It is said that with the calculation of the decimal method and in the name of the one (1), the distinguished *Virat Purusha* (the primordial man) being attached with the zero (0), becomes ten-finger larger than the universe. The *mantra* also says that the *Virat Purusha* bears one-thousand heads, one-thousand eyes and one-thousand feet.

सहस्रशीर्षा पुरुषः सहस्राक्षः सहस्रपात्।
स भूमिं विश्वतो वृत्वात्यतिष्ठद्दशाङ्गुलम्॥

—ऋग्वेद (10.90.1)

[Translation: The *Purusha* (Universal Being) has thousand heads, He has thousand eyes, He has thousand feet, and He envelops the World from all sides, and is beyond the count with ten fingers.]

The apparent effect of the decimal method can be seen in the above-mentioned *mantra* of *The Rigveda*. The seers of *The Veda*s gave us the idea of the creation of the universe from the elements of *ka* (one) and *kha* (zero); they first invented the decimal system of mathematics from these elements. The following *mantra*s[1, 2] in *The Rigveda* also confirm the decimal number system:

न सहस्राय नायुताय वज्रिवो

न शताय शतामघ

—ऋग्वेद (8.1.5)

ये ते सन्ति दशग्विनः शतिनो

ये सहस्रिणः

—ऋग्वेद (8.1.9)

It is true that *Aryabhatta* created a few important formulae to connect the decimal system with pure mathematics, but it is for certain that *Aryabhata* was not the original inventor of this decimal theory; long before him the existence of decimal method in Indian civilization can be found in Vedic literature. In this context we have mentioned two *mantra*s from *The Rigveda* as above, where decimal numbers like ten (दश), one-hundred (शत), one-thousand (सहस्र), and so on can be found. Let us now forget *The Veda*s. We cannot, under any circumstances, ignore *The Ramayana* that told us that *Ravana* got ten heads, and he was thus called *Dashananah* (one who bears ten heads). Again, in *The Mahabharata* we were told of the one-hundred *Kaurava*s. Both these scriptures had been written much before *Aryabhatta* was born. We can, therefore, certainly question the authenticity of the claim that *Aryabhatta* invented or discovered the zero around 500 AD.

With the rise and subsequent fall of the civilizations the principles and formulations changed accordingly. The sun does not get destroyed even after it sets in the west. Without the existence of the zero and the decimal system it seems impossible to calculate mathematically. But in *The Vedas* we can find the mention of ten-thousand, one-lac, ten-lac, one-crore, ten-crore, one-arab, ten-arab, one-trillion (*kharab*), ten-trillion (ten-*kharab*), one-*nil* (ten times of ten-trillion), ten-*nil*, one-*shankh*, ten-*shankh,* and so on, the highest number being *parardha* (one-lac crore). These numbers are suggestive of the then decimal system of mathematics.

Notes: *Mantras*[1, 2]

महे चन त्वामद्रिवः परा शुल्काय देयाम्।
न सहस्राय नायुताय वज्रिवो न शताय शतामघ॥

—ऋग्वेद (8.1.5)

[Translation: O thunder-bearer *Indra*, I don't sell you at any cost. Nor would I sell you against a fee of one-thousand or ten-thousand possessions. O priceless, I won't sell you against an infinite price either.]

ये ते सन्ति दशग्विनः शतिनो ये सहस्रिणः।
अश्वासो ये ते वृषणो रघुद्रुवस्तेभिर्नस्तूयमा गहि॥

—ऋग्वेद (8.1.9)

[Translation: O *Indra*, the horses you own range from one-hundred to one-thousand in number and they run a distance of ten-*Yojana* (576 kilometers approx) quite fast and they are capable of cultivating the land. Please arrive soon riding on your horses.]

From the One to the One-Lac Crore

From the historic and archaeological evidences it has been documented that the decimal method was first invented by the Vedic Aryans who worshiped Mother Nature. The numbers did not remain confined within the scriptures; they were also used for calculating things in the Vedic times. Measurement tools have been found in the Indus-Valley civilization, the most ancient civilization of the Aryans. Again, Mohenjo-Daro and Harappa civilizations convey us the evidence of the decimal method that was traditionally employed in business transactions in those times. An expert scholar, Dr. Mackay, by examining the measurement of a 6.62-inch-long conch of Indus-Valley civilization, has stated that the traces for measuring the length of this unit were of 0.264-inch and bore five sections of 1.32-inch tall. On this basis Mackay had speculated that the prehistoric resident of the Indus-Valley was aware of the decimal system.

Literature is the mirror of our society, and the same is true with Vedic literature as well. It can be said that the decimal method and the zero existed even before the Vedic period. Supporting evidences can be found in *The Rigveda*, *The Yajurveda*, etc. *The Yajurveda* suggests the use of different decimal numbers in a certain sequence. For example:

इमा मे अग्न

इष्टका धेनव: सन्त्वेका च दश च दश च शतं च शतं च सहसं च सहसं चायुतं चायुतं च नियुतं च नियुतं च प्रयुतं चार्बुदं च न्यर्बुदं च समुद्रश्च मध्यं चान्तश्च परार्धश्चैता मे अग्न इष्टका धेनव: सन्त्वमुत्रामुष्मिंल्लोके॥

—शुक्ल-यजुर्वेद, वाजसनेयी संहिता (17.2)

[Translation: O God *Agni!* May these bricks (used to construct the firepot, *yajnakunda*) bring the desired results as does the *Kamadhenu* (a divine cow, who was praised by the sages, for milk and/or prosperity) to us. May these bricks become larger: from one to ten, from ten to one-hundred, from one-hundred to one-thousand, from one-thousand to ten-thousand, from ten-thousand to one-lac, from one-lac to ten-lac, from ten-lac to one-crore, from one-crore to ten-crore, from ten-crore to one-arab, from one-arab to ten-arab, from ten-arab to one-kharab, from one-kharab to ten-khrab, from ten-khrab to one-nil, from one-nil to ten-nil, from ten-nil to one-*shankha*, from one-*shankha* to ten-*shankha*, and from ten-*shankha* to the number *parardha* (one-lac crore). May these bricks be mine own *kamadhenu* (milch-kine) in yonder world and in this world.]

A similar list[1] is also available in *Taittiriiya-Sanhita* of *Krishna-Yajurveda* (4.4.11 and 7.2.20), *Maitrayani-Sanhita* (2.8.4), *Kathaka-Sanhita*, (17.10), etc. *The Atharvaveda*[2] (6.25.1-3, 7.4.1) emphasizes on the common relationship between one and ten, three and thirty, five and fifty, nine and ninety, and thus, clearly indicating that the persons of the Vedic age had a fair command on the basics of the decimal system for positive integers.

Such large numbers, as derived from the decimal method, are not found in the history of any other ancient civilization, except for the Vedic civilization. The Greeks failed to use large numbers because they could not write the numbers with the help of letters, on the other hand ancient India not only invented but also named them all.

After the invention of the zero in the era of Vedic texts, there was knowledge of the numbers, from one-to-nine. The Vedic Aryans started calculating the digits from the zero and the tenth digit coming after the nine was considered to be a complete unit of number one. Hence, the sages of *The Upanishad*s had given the noun as पूर्ण (complete). Here the zero is an indicator of the completeness of one digit, and then it is the starting point of the second unit. According to Indian Cosmology there have been several turmoil followed by destruction of the universe. And the universe has been re-created after every destruction. This phenomenon has resemblance with the decimal method that we use even now. For example, in the mathematical theories of Vedic literature, finishing the calculation of the number one (1) after the zero (0), the counting of the

second number begins immediately, and it
runs from the one (1) to the nine (9).

Notes:

List[1]

अग्नेरन्तः ...इमा मे अग्न इष्टका धेनवः ...
कामदुघा अमुत्रामुष्मिंल्लोके॥

—कृष्ण-यजुर्वेद, तैत्तिरीय संहिता (4.4.11)

शताय स्वाहा सहस्राय स्वाहा...परार्धाय स्वाहोषसे
स्वाहा॥

—कृष्ण-यजुर्वेद, तैत्तिरीय संहिता (7.2.20)

आशुस्त्रिवृ,...योनिश्चतुर्विंशः,...चतुष्टोमः॥

—कृष्ण-यजुर्वेद, मैत्रायणी संहिता (2.8.4)

आयोस्त्वा सदने...सहस्रस्य प्रमासि सहस्रस्य
प्रतिमासि सहस्रस्योन्मासि...कामदुघास्ता मे अग्र
इष्टका धेनवस्सन्तु॥

—कृष्ण-यजुर्वेद, काठक संहिता (17.10)

पञ्च च याः पञ्चाशच्च संयन्ति मन्या अभि।
इतस्ताः सर्वा नश्यन्तु वाका अपचितामिव॥
—अथर्ववेद (6.25.1)

सप्त च याः सप्ततिश्च संयन्ति ग्रैव्या अभि।
इतस्ताः सर्वा नश्यन्तु वाका अपचितामिव॥
–अथर्ववेद (6.25.2)

नव च या नवतिश्च संयन्ति स्कन्ध्या अभि।
इतस्ताः सर्वा नश्यन्तु वाका अपचितामिव॥
—अथर्ववेद (6.25.3)

एकया च दशभिश्चा सुहुते द्वाभ्यामिष्टये विंशत्या
च।
तिसृभिश्च वहसे त्रिंशता च वियुग्भिर्वाय इह ता वि
मुञ्च॥
—अथर्ववेद (7.4.1)

Naming the Numbers

After the invention of the decimal method, the only need was to invent the numbers from one to nine, so we could make further numbers. If we explore the mathematical clues laid in every name given to a particular number, we will understand how prosperous India remained in terms of Mathematics and Philosophy in the Vedic period. The number, eleven was named *ekadasa* (एकादश) [*Eka* (एक) means one, and *dasa* (दश) indicates ten]. Similarly, the number, twelve, was named *dwadasa* (द्वादश) [*Dwa* is derived from *dwi* (द्वि) that means two, and *dasa* (दश) means ten]. Again, the number, twenty-one, was named *ekabinsati* (एकविंशति) which involved the addition of twenty or *binsati* (विंशति) with one or *eka* (एक). In *The Atharvaveda*[1] (19.23.16) the usage of the number nineteen can be traced by the name *ekonabinsati* (एकोनविंशति), which means one [=*eka* (एक)] less [=*una* (उन)] twenty [=*binsati* (विंशति)]. In

57

Vajasaneyi Sanhita[2] (14.30) of *The Shukla-Yajurveda*, *nabadasa* [नवदश= nine/*naba* (नव) + ten/*dasa* (दश)] has been used for the number nineteen. In *The Rigveda*[3] (1.84.13) *navatinava* (नवतिनव) has been used for the number ninety-nine (99) [नवति= ninety and नव= nine].

Finally, this has been observed that two types of mathematical calculations were there to represent numbers using the decimal method, one in a positive way, and the other in a negative direction. And the decimal method has been the core factor. For example, the number nineteen (19) has expressed in both ways like 10 + 9 [नवदश= nine/*naba* (नव) + ten/*dasa* (दश)] and 20-1 (उनविंशति= less/ उन, twenty/ विंशति).

Notes:

The Atharvaveda[1] (19.23.16):

एकोनविंशांतिः स्वाहा॥

Vajasaneyi Samhita[2] (14.30):

नवदशभिरस्तुवत्...एवाधिपतय आसन्।

The Rigveda[3] (1.84.13):

इन्द्रो दधीचो अस्थभिर्वृत्राण्यप्रतिष्कुतः।

जघान नवतीर्नव॥

From Completeness to Nothingness

Some Western scholars think the decimal system, as found in *Brahmanical* texts (an important part of the Vedic literature), has been influenced by the Greeks, but they have failed to prove the antiquity of the Greeks in comparison with the Vedic Aryans. The numbers that bore only three or four zeros could be seen in the Greek and Roman texts (3rd century AD). This indicates that the Greeks and Romans were capable of counting numbers only up to ten-thousand. *The Vedas* were far ahead in this regard, as we mentioned before.

Some Indian scholars believe that the decimal system was propagated from India to other countries like Indonesia, China, etc in the 6th century AD. Most of the scholars of the Western world tried to prove that the zero was invented in the middle of the 5th century AD for the first time. There is another misconception: *Digambar Jain Muni Sarvanandi* first introduced the zero as mentioned in the book, *Lokabibhaga*, written in the *Prakrit-*

language. The decimal number system was also mentioned in this book. In 498 AD the Indian mathematician, *Aryabhatta*, claimed in his book, *Aryabhatiya*, that when the number, one (1) became ten (10) its value increased by ten times. Similarly, when the number, ten (10) became one-hundred (100) the value got 10-time higher. *Aryabhatta* named the units accordingly:

एकं दश च शतं च सहस्रमयुतनियुते तथा प्रयुतम्।
कोट्यार्बुदं च वृन्दं स्थानात् स्थानं दशगुणं स्यात्॥

—आर्यभटीय, गणितपाद (2)

1 = **एक** (one unit)

10 = **दश** (ten-unit)

100 = **शत** (hundred-unit)

1000 = **सहस्र** (thousand-unit)

10,000 = **अयुत** (ten-thousand)

1,00,000 = **नियुत** (lac-unit)

10,00,000 = **प्रयुत** (million-unit)

100,00,000 = **कोटि** (crore-unit)

10,00,00,000 = **अर्बुद** (ten-crore)

100,00,00,000 = **वृन्द** (arab unit)

The nomenclature, as proposed by *Aryabhatta,* is assumed to be the origin of the decimal principle of the numbers. But, the same nomenclature existed before in *The Shukla-Yajurveda*[1] (17.2) as we have discussed earlier. Again, the zero was used in ancient *Bukshali* manuscript. Although the exact time (the period when it was written) of the manuscript is not known to us, but this is for sure that *Bukshali* manuscript was composed much before *Aryabhatiya.*

In seventh century AD the unpredictable use of the zero and the decimal method can also be found in *The Brahmasphutasidhhanta* written by *Brahmagupta,* who is considered the inventor of the zero by many scholars. But, the zero existed before *Brahmagupta* wrote his book. However, the use of the negative numbers and algebraic theories in this book was remarkable. During 7th century AD, the concept of the zero reached Cambodia, and only a few documents suggest that it propagated from Cambodia to China, and then to other Muslim countries. The scholars might have messed up with facts, as the time period was in close approximation with the times of *Brahmagupta*.

Differences between Vedic and Jain doctrines are also seen when it comes to dividing a number by the zero. *Sridhara* had written in his book *Trishatika* that while dividing the zero by the zero, the result would be zero, but the Jain mathematician *Mahavira* had written in his *Ganitsarasangraha* that the zero remained unchanged.

ताडितः खेन राशिः खं सोऽविकारी हृतो युतः।
हीनोऽपि खवधादिः खं योगे खं योज्यरूपकम्॥
—गणितसारसंग्रहः (संज्ञाधिकारः 49)

It can be said in favor of *Mahavira* that if we divide the number twenty by the number four the result will be five. But, if the same number, twenty is divided by the zero, no change will occur. It is logical to say 'unchanged' as the number twenty remains as-it-is. In the same context *Bhaskaracharya* coined the name *Khahara*.

While discussing the mathematics of the zero in his book titled *Bijaganitam*, *Bhaskaracharya* explained *khahara* as a quantity derived from dividing a number by the zero:

...खहरो भवेत् खेनभक्तश्च राशिः।

—भास्करीयबीजगणितम् (3)

A relevant question can be found in his discussion further:

द्विघ्नं त्रिहृत् खं खहृतं त्रयं च।

शून्यस्य वर्गं वद मे पदं च॥

—भास्करीयबीजगणितम् (उदाहरणम्-5, P-15)

The *sholka* says: What will happen if two is multiplied by zero or three is divided by zero? Tell me; what are the root and the square-root of the zero?

It is difficult to set a definite stand regarding those questions. It is impossible to address them properly. However, as *Bhaskaracharya* continued, the infinite (*ananta*) quantity (2×0 or $3/0$) is called *khahara:* अयमनन्तो राशिः खहरः इत्युच्यते

[*Nyasa*, a commentary on भास्करीय-बीजगणितम्, P-15]

Bhaskaracharya argued that if we add any number to this *Khahara* or deduct any number from it, there would be no change in *Khahara*; as God remains 'eternal' and 'unchanged' in the times of creation of the universe or its destruction. No wonder *Khahara* is called 'infinite' by the mathematicians of modern times.

अस्मिन्निकारः खहरे न राशावपि प्रविष्टेष्वपि

निःसृतेषु।

बहुष्वपिस्याल्लयसृष्टिकालेऽनन्तेऽच्युते भूतगणेषु

यद्वत्॥

—भास्करीयबीजगणितम् (4)

[Translation: In this quantity *khahara*, there is no alteration even if many are added or taken out, just as there is no alteration in the infinite (*ananta*), infallible (*acyuta*/ *lord Vishnu*/ *Brahma*) even though many groups of beings enter in or emanate from (It) at times of dissolution and creation.]

The Vedic mathematicians believed that God was the only truth and eternal;

but the view of *Bhaskaracharya* about God held no merit for the Jain philosophers, who did not believe in the existence of God. This was the reason why the Jain mathematician *Mahavira* didn't consider *Khahara* as infinite. In this context "unchanged" seemed more appropriate according to *Mahavira*.

Later the symbol of the *Brahma*, *kha*, became an alphabetic sign for the zero in Indian mathematics. On the other hand, people started to worship *kha* as the symbol of immense power (in *tantravidya text*). The *Tantric*s added trigonometry into mathematics during their foray into worshipping the power. In *Kamdhenutantra* the mention of worshiping *kha* can be found; here *kha* is the mathematical expression of the triangle and the zero.

खकारं परमाश्चर्यं शङ्खकुन्दसमप्रभम्।
कोणत्रययुतं शून्यं बिन्दुत्रयसमन्वितम्॥
गुणत्रययुतं देवि! पञ्चदेवमयं सदा।
त्रिशक्तिसंयुतं वर्णं खकारं प्रणमाम्यहम्॥

—शब्दकल्पद्रुम

[Translation: *kha* is a strange letter having been brightened by the jasmines and conch-shells. It is associated with the triangle, null or void (the zero) and the three points. It is the goddess bearing three divine virtues, and housing the five gods. I pay my obeisance to the letter, *kha*, which holds the three enormous powers, *tri-shakti*.]

The Vedic literature is not a theoretical book on Mathematics. *The Veda*s deal with the supreme wisdom. In the context of the decimal method it can be said that the definition of the decimal method may not be found in *The Veda*s, but the decimal numbers were used in the Vedic *Sanhitas* (collections of *mantra*s) for many a time, followed by the decimal principles. Proper sequence of the decimal numbers can be found in *The Rigveda*[2] (8.1.5) and *The Yajurveda*[3] (17.2). However, the decimal method was found to be fully developed during the time of *Brahmanical* text.

The world came to know about the zero which was invented by the *Vedic Aryans* in India. The zero has influenced the numerical mathematics of the whole world with the decimal method. The very first use of the decimal method can be found in *The Veda*s that is essentially an Indian scripture. The Middle East countries and other civilizations of rest of the world obtained the zero from the ancient Indian scholars. This concept of the zero of ancient India reached everywhere until the 12th century AD. The zero that now indicates nothingness or void was primarily intended to mean fullness or completeness by the Vedic Aryans. The absolutist zero of India has become *sifr* (empty) in the Arabian countries. And then, through Latin (*cipher/cephirum*), European (*zephyrum*), Italian (*zefiro/zevero*), and French (*zéro*) civilizations the *sifr* became the zero in the English-language.

Notes:

The Shukla Yajurveda[1] (17.2): See page 52.

The Rigveda[2] (8.1.5) and *The Yajurveda*[3] (17.2): See pages 49 and 52.

The Real Numbers

The natural numbers (1, 2, 3, etc.) indicate an amount, quantity or measurement. But, why would someone use or invent a figure that indicates nothingness or emptiness? Funny! The real numbers (1, 2, 3, etc.) are the ones that occur naturally while counting on the presence of a substance. Emptiness is amorphous, while the zero aids in counting. People count on the numbers to quantify the things they intend to measure. Hence, no number or figure was needed to measure emptiness in the first place.

The Zero in Yoga

The zero is the only number that cannot stand alone. It is a lonely number, lonelier than one. It requires some sort of companionship to add meaning to its life. It can go on the left, on the right or in the middle as part of a threesome. See: "01," "10," or "102." A certain relationship with other numbers gives the zero a meaning.

Yoga is the union of human soul with the divine soul. And it aids in realizing the self. We often refer the action to as *Rajyoga* or *Kriyayoga* which is based on *Patanjal Yoga Sutras* that emphasize on the three *Nadi*s situated around the human spine: *Ida*, *Pingala* and *Sushumna*.

The yogis use their *Sushumna Nadi* which has the six centers, spiritually known as *Shat-Chakra*. All these centers are represented by a lotus with varied number of petals. But it is at the *Kutastha* where a yogi envisions the *Jyoti* (divine light) and merges completely with the Supreme Being. They say *Kutastha* is located on the forehead, right at the middle of the eyebrows. And it is the *Kutastha* that holds the zero: Here zero is not a number, but nothingness or *kha* (as we discussed before), representing the *Brahma*.

The yogis say there is another zero in the core of the zero at *Kutastha*. And it's the inner zero where a yogi intends to remain for the lifetime. It is to be remembered that the communion of the two souls (human and divine) takes place in the zero and results in one: Here one is not a number, but the being.

Conclusion

In this book I wanted to explore that like other branches of science, invention of the zero was first made by the Vedic sages and scholars in ancient India. Many scholars of Mathematics are still unaware of, or ignorant about the fact that the Vedic Aryans in ancient India invented the concept of the zero on the surface of universal science or cosmology, and later this invention turned out to be a milestone in the field of Mathematics.

We need to understand that if there was no zero (here zero means nothingness), no creation could have occurred, nor had the creation become the world. Mathematics is said to be the language to express the sciences of this universe, and 'zero' has its unique stand and glory in Mathematics. Subsequently the entire numerology and statistics were developed from the decimal method which originated from the zero. Therefore, civilizations across the world should remain grateful to the Vedic Aryans for their invention of the zero and decimal method.

It is a pity that Indian academic curriculum barely reserves a place for the scholars in ancient India; the ones who made the entire world aware of the various facets of wisdom. This is probably the reason that the great scholars like *Varahmihira*, *Aryabhatta*, *Brahmagupta*, *Bhaskaracharya*, *Mahavira*, among others are often ignored in the prestigious academic institutions in India. Due to the Western influence there have been persistent efforts to tampering historical facts. Every possible effort should be extended to retrieve and restore historical data for the sake of mankind.

Acknowledgements

I'm eternally grateful to my family, which is comprised of my wife, Kalpita Acharya, and parents: Naresh Chandra Acharya and Archana Acharya, and my older brother, Somen Acharya.

Let me express my gratitude to all my teachers and resource persons of Sanskrit language and literature, including Prof. Raghunath Ghosh, Prof. Gopal Chandra Mishra, Prof. Rita Chattopadhyay, Prof. Sarbani Ganguly, Prof. Ratna Basu, Prof. Tapan Sankar Bhattacharya, Prof. Kalpika Mukhopadhyay, Prof. Kakoli Ghosh, Prof. Ayan Bhattacharya, Prof. Didhiti Biswas, Prof. Mou Das Gupta, Prof. Piyali Praharaj, and Prof. Taraknath Adhikary, among others for sharing their wisdom in every possible way. They all have left profound impact on my mind.

Heartfelt thanks to Kiriti Sengupta for his unconditional love, wholehearted support and precious time. Can I thank him enough? He has not only named this book, he has offered necessary edits and inputs from time to time.

Sources and Suggested Reading

Rigveda-Sanhita, translated from its original Sanskrit by Ramesh Chandra Dutta, and edited by Nimai Chandra Pal (2007, Sadesh Publishers, Calcutta)

Chhandogya Upanishad, English translation by Swami Nikhilananda (E-book)

Sriharivakyasudhasindhoh: Srikrishnavallavacharya. First edition 1979 Chowkhamba, Varanasi, India

Shabdakalpadrum: Radha Kanta Deva. Part 5, Third edition 1967 Chowkhamba, Varanasi, India

The Hymns of the Rigveda, translated by Ralph T. H. Griffith, Second edition 1896, Kotagiri (Nilgiri), India

Ganita-Sara-Sangraha: Mahaviracharya. English translations and notes by M.Rangacarya. 1912 Government Press, Madras (now Chennai), India

Bijganit (Elements of Algebra): Bhaskaracharya, edited by Deva Chandra Jha. First Edition 1983, Krishnadas Academy, Varanasi, India

Vajasaneyi Madhyandina Shukla Yajurveda Samhitayah Sarvanukrama Sutram, Chowkhamba Sanskrit Series Office, Varanasi, India

Chhandogya Upanisad, E-book, Part 1-8

Krishna-Yajurvediya Taittariya-Sanhita, edited by Narayan Sharma and Trivikram Sharma. Part 1, Volume I (E-book), Vaidik-Sangshadhan-Mandala, Maharastra, India

Vedic Selections (Part II), edited by Prof. Bhabaniprasad Bhattacharya and Prof. Taraknath Adhikary, First Edition 2001, Sanskrit Book Depot., Kolkata, India

wikipedia dot com

sacredtexts dot com

indigyan dot blogspot dot in

paravigyan dot com

Annexure

Environment Consciousness in Ancient India

*The Veda*s are the first texts in the literature of human race. They deal with knowledge, both physical and spiritual. The Vedic views revolve around the concept of Nature and life. We can easily figure it out how nature was related to life and livelihood of Vedic people through their literature which is referred to as *The Veda*s. This paper attempts to explore the awareness of ancient Indian people about Environment. In various texts of *The Veda*s we find the oldest and simplest form of Nature worship. This ancient literature reflects on the history of Vedic period, as literature mirrors society and social lives.

*The Veda*s are filled with strong statements, various ideas and unusual images, which contain factual truths of the universe. Again, if modern science is observed through the lens of Vedic philosophy, different fraternities of science can be reached at their primary or primitive forms. The Vedic sages gave complete descriptions of all the disciplines which have been developed and taught down the ages.

Modern science defines Environment as follows: Environment includes water, air, and land, and their inter-relationship with human beings, other living creatures, plants, micro-organisms and property (both movable and immovable).[*Ref: The Environment Protection Act, 1986*] According to this definition, Environment consists of two components namely, living beings and non-living beings.

According to *The Atharvaveda* there are three covers of the environment and they are referred to as *Chandaṃsi*. They are: Water, Air and Herbs. They exist in the world since the birth of the planet: "*trīṇi ca chandāṃsi kavayo bi yetire pururūpaṃ darśataṃ viśvacakṣaṃ/ āpo vātā ouṣadhayastānyekasmin bhubana arpitāni*" (*The Atharvaveda* 18.1.17). It proves the Vedic sages had enough knowledge and understanding of the basic elements of the environment. On the other hand, *The Upaniṣads* describe earth, air, ether, water and light as the five basic elements of the universe: "*imāni pañcamahābhūtāni pṛthivī vāyuḥ ākāśaḥ āpjyotīṣī"* (*The Aitareya Upaniṣad* 3.3).

Any disturbance/abnormality in them disturbs the natural balance that influences the living creatures. The relation between human and Environment is believed to be very strong as human race can't live without Mother Nature. People in the Vedic period were intimately attached to Nature. *"māta bhūmiḥ putro ahaṃ pṛthivyāḥ"*—The earth is my mother and I'm her son (*The Atharvaveda* 12.1.12). They observed and understood natural hazards like heavy rainfall, lightening, storm, tremendous heat of the sun, draught, flood, etc. The Vedic sages felt the greatness of Nature, but failed to comprehend the exact reasons behind natural calamities. *The Veda*s are not a literature of a single era; rather, it had been edited (through inclusions) down the ages. It was around 6000 BC when *The Veda*s existed in verbal form, as the skill of writing had not been discovered in those days. According to MaxMullar, the Vedic literature had been completed (as in its present form) at around 1200 BC. Weber proposed a different view. According to him it was around 4000BC that marked the completion of the Vedic literature. Naturally, the ideas and beliefs changed in every era.

The Vedic sages were confused and worshipped Nature out of surprise and fear at the very beginning of the Vedic period, but then at the *Upaniṣadic* period they tried to realize them and opened up their vision to know the original facts.

The hymns of *The Rigveda* relate to natural forces. They describe the gods as remaining under the influence of the most impressive phenomenon of nature and its several aspects. The attributes assigned to the gods fit in their natural forms and activities. For example, the fire is bright, the air is fast-moving, the sun is the destroyer of darkness, and so on.

We can't ignore the importance of water in our daily life. The water plays a pivotal role in balancing our environment since the formation of the earth. *Indra* is commonly known as *Vritrahantā* (the one who killed *Vritra*) in *The Vedas*. *Vritra* was a demon who fetched draught. On the other hand, *Indra*, the god who brought rain, was able to kill that demon by his powerful weapon *Vajra*, otherwise called thunder. This natural but scientific phenomenon of Nature has been elaborated throughout the verses in *Rigvedic* hymn 1.32. The Vedic people perhaps worshipped *Indra* to get rid of draught and to secure sufficient water for their living. The Vedic sages prayed boldly to these natural forces to protect themselves and for their prosperity. Although they were apprehensive of natural disasters and extreme climatic conditions, the Vedic sages turned up as experts in Nature science.

One of the most enchanting verses of *The Rigveda* says: Heaven is my father, brother atmosphere is my navel, and the great earth is my mother— "*dyaurme pitā janitā nābhiratra bandhurme mātā pṛthivī mahīyam*" (*The Rigveda* 1.164.33). The famous hymn called *the Bhūmisuktam* in *The Atharvaveda* indicates environmental consciousness of Vedic seers. *Bhūmi* or *Pṛthivī* (earth) is our mother. She is called *Vasudhā* for containing all wealth, *Hiraṇyavakṣa* for bearing gold, *Niveshāni* for being abode of the whole world, *Visvambharā* for her representation on behalf of the universe. It is also believed that the earth is not meant only for the human beings, but also for other creatures on this planet—*"tvaṃ bibharṣi dvipadaḥ tvaṃ catuṣpadaḥ"* (*The Atharvaveda* 12.1.15). Animals and birds are also a part of Nature and environment. *The Rigveda* classifies these creatures into three groups: sky animals (bird, bat, etc.), forest animals (tiger, wolf, etc.) and animals in human habitations (cow, horse, etc.)— *"paśuntaṃścakre vāyavyānārāṇyan gāmyāśca je"* (*The Rigveda* 10.90). They all have importance in various ways, and they have an environment of their own.

There is a general feeling in the Vedic verses that animals should be safe, protected and healthy. Domestic animals like cows, horses as well as wild animals along with human beings should live in peace under the protection of the gods like *Pūṣan*. The cow occupies a very important role in ancient Indian civilization. The cows have been treated as *Gomātā* and well respected for their varied utilities in domestic life (*The Yajurveda* 19.20, 3.37 & *The Atharvaveda* 11.2.24).

The Vedic seers had a good knowledge of various herbs. In *The Atharvaveda* we can see the significance and usage of different herbs. *Ayurveda* which is a part of *The Atharvaveda* is all about the medicinal properties of various herbs and the cure of different illness by using those herbs. Throughout this important part of the Vedic literature, the herbs are explained as protector of human body and soul.

Aranyani Suktam of *The Rigveda* strongly urges that the forest should always be green with trees and plants. In modern medical science there are different, definite ways to cure a disease, but it was not like that before. The ancient Indian people depended on forests to cure themselves from diseases and in order to keep the body and mind healthy they used to meditate in ashrams that were surrounded by greenery. They were well aware of the fact that plants came earlier than the animals here in this earth—*"ya ouṣadhīḥ pūrvā jātā devebhyastriyugaṃ purā"* (*The Rigveda* 10.97.1). This surprises us owing to the fact that the ancient people were aware of the scientific trait of evolution without any equipment.

Modern scientists should feel proud of our ancestors for their profound understanding and views on Environment. Ancient Indian sages knew about various aspects of Environment (*Prithivi*- earth,

Vayu- the air, *Apah-the water*, *Teja*-the fire and *Aakasha*-the sky), and also the importance of coordination between all natural powers. During prayer the sages expressed their beliefs of the interrelationship among these extreme powers. Prayers carry lives within, they strongly believed that the natural powers existed — their thoughts, these powers and the sages praised them too.

Environment consciousness in ancient India has been documented in Vedic literature. *The Veda*s have urged that Environment belongs to all living beings, so it deserves to be protected by all of us. If we take care for our environment, it will give us years to live here in this earth. The ancient people wished to live a life of a hundred-year—*"jīvema śaradaḥ śatam"* (*The Atharvaveda* 19.67.1), and they were aware of the fact that Environment should essentially be kept pollution-free, clean and peaceful.

Note: The article first appeared on *The Tuck Magazine* on October 18, 2016.
http://tuckmagazine.com/2016/10/18/enviro nment-consciousness-ancient-india/